Contents

Introduction

Exploring dance and movement

Dance and movement contribute to a child's educational experience and should take place in a safe, disciplined environment. This book builds upon children's natural enthusiasm for physical activity, giving them the opportunity to explore what their bodies can do.

This book describes how to use a range of stimuli such as action rhymes, stories, pictures, music and props to help children respond in a variety of ways to what they see and hear. The activities provide the opportunity for children to express and communicate ideas, thoughts and feelings as they explore and understand the meaning of dance.

Learning through activity and interaction, children will develop a variety of skills, be able to carry out tasks, make decisions and solve problems. They will be encouraged to think about the story behind their dance and make connections with other areas of the curriculum as they compose, perform, appreciate and evaluate dance.

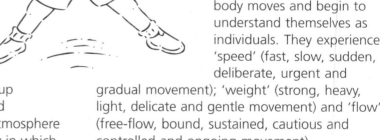

Movement sessions

Purposeful, safe and enjoyable warm-up activities prepare children mentally and physically for action. They create an atmosphere of calm, trust, co-operation and safety in which children gain confidence, acclimatize to the space and establish relationships. Cooling down helps children to recover by gently reducing physical and mental activity levels before reviewing, reflecting and evaluating the task.

The language of dance and movement

The activities in this book expose children to a rich movement vocabulary based upon how the body moves, what can be moved, where it can move and with whom. This helps children to understand what is happening to them when they move. They will hear and use the language of travel by hopping, skipping, running, crawling, shuffling and sliding; of jumping as they leap, bounce, soar, spring, hop and fly, and of turning and spinning as they twist, twirl, roll, unwind, spiral and pivot. Through the gestures of stamping, punching, reaching, opening and closing, leaning and waving, pointing and wagging, children learn about non-verbal communication, experiencing stillness, how to wait, pause, hold a movement, freeze and suspend movement in time.

The activities in this book cover 'space' (personal and general); 'direction' (up, down, right, left, forward, backward and diagonally); 'size' (big and little); 'pathways' in space (straight, meandering, curved, angular, zigzag and spiral) and 'body shapes' (tuck, curl, stretch and symmetrical and asymmetrical twists).

Children explore how the body moves and begin to understand themselves as individuals. They experience 'speed' (fast, slow, sudden, deliberate, urgent and gradual movement); 'weight' (strong, heavy, light, delicate and gentle movement) and 'flow' (free-flow, bound, sustained, cautious and controlled and ongoing movement).

The Early Learning Goals

Through the ideas in this book, children discover how to use new skills in dance and movement activities linked to the Early Learning Goals (QCA) for Physical development and Creative development. They will gain confidence, feel the positive benefits of being healthy and active, and develop a sense of well-being.

The ideas are equally applicable to the documents on pre-school education published for Scotland, Wales and Northern Ireland.

With this book, children will learn to:
- move confidently, imaginatively and safely
- talk to other children about their actions
- explore different ways of representing ideas and actions
- repeat and change actions, think about, refine, change and improve them
- move with control and co-ordination
- travel around, under, over and through balancing equipment
- show awareness of space, of themselves and of others
- recognize the importance of being healthy and what that means
- recognize the changes that happen to their bodies when active
- use a range of equipment
- handle a variety of objects safely and with increasing control.

Baseline Assessment
The activities in this book will help to develop skills in young children that will enable them to achieve the Early Learning Goals by the end of the Reception Year. This will also enable them to carry out the Baseline Assessment tasks that they will be expected to carry out when they enter mainstream school.

How to use this book
This book provides a framework of ideas to use flexibly according to the needs and abilities of children and the curriculum of individual settings. It is not intended that you follow the activities in the order of presentation. Observe the children to discover particular needs and interests before adapting the activities to suit.

Give them time to experiment with different forms of response so that they feel at home with themselves and discover individual creativity. There is no right or wrong way to respond.

Celebrate unique, individual ways of moving to give all the children the opportunity to experience success. As confidence grows, encourage the children to describe and demonstrate their dance capabilities to others. Arrange dance performances to provide added challenges.

For each activity, there are suggestions for assessing the children's attainment and progress, and for simplifying or extending the activity to meet the needs of individual children.

Each activity is supported with a photocopiable sheet. Where a sheet is to be used by individual children, the activity is referred to as 'Individual recording', for example, 'Row the boat' on page 8. Where a photocopiable sheet is to be used jointly by a group of children, then the activity is referred to as an 'Individual task', for example, 'Teddy lost, Teddy found' on page 14.

The Skills development chart can be used to record what the children can do and understand in dance and movement. The example on page 32 is a starting-point from which practitioners can develop their own designs according to the assessment, planning and record-keeping requirements of their settings.

Home links
This section offers practical ways to encourage support for the children's learning at home. Parents and carers are invited to follow their children's development to help them grow in confidence and gain mastery of movement.

Freeze

Learning objectives
To move with confidence and in safety; to move with control and co-ordination; to show an awareness of space; to stop on command.

Group size
Any size.

What you need
The photocopiable sheet; large, safe space; floor mats; three different-coloured marker pens for each child.

Preparation
Make a copy of the photocopiable sheet for each child. Encourage the children to place the floor mats in a space. Invite them to warm up for the activity by quietly jogging on their mats. Ask them to stretch up high and then curl up in a ball on their mats. Repeat several times.

What to do
Invite the children to sit on the mats. Discuss the importance of responding to safety signals in case of accidents or emergency. Point out the need to move around carefully to avoid bumping into anyone. Tell the children that when you say 'Freeze!' they must stop and stand still until you tell them to move again. Invite them to walk around the mats. Encourage them to use all the space. Call out 'Freeze!' at random intervals. Repeat until all the children fully understand the concept.

Invite the children to increase their speed to a jogging pace between the 'Freeze!' commands. Challenge the children to run around all the mats. Remind them to be careful and to stop instantly on the command of 'Freeze!'.

Invite the children to calm down at the end of the session by gradually decreasing their speed to a slow walking pace. Ask them to return to their mats. Finish by stretching and curling. Talk about the activity with the children while they are sitting on their mats.

Individual recording
Give each child a copy of the photocopiable sheet. Invite them to use different-coloured markers to draw the pathways that they took around the mats when they were walking, jogging and running.

Support
Invite younger children to show you with their fingers the pathways that they took, before drawing them with the pens.

Extension
Encourage older children to plan different routes for the various speeds on their photocopiable sheets using different-coloured pens.

Assessment
Note the children's ability to use the space. Can they put the mats into a space? Note whether they can move around the mats without touching them. Do they stop instantly on command? Can they differentiate between walking, jogging and running fast? Note whether the children can avoid bumping into one another.

Home links
Let the children take home the photocopiable sheet to explain the activity to their parents and carers. Ask them to choose a special word together instead of 'Freeze!' to use at home. Invite them to add the word to a list to compare different ways of saying 'stop'.

Freeze

Cat's coming!

Learning objective
To move with confidence, imagination and in safety using the contrasting speeds of fast and slow.

Group size
Any size.

What you need
The photocopiable sheet; large, safe space; selection of nursery rhyme books containing pictures and traditional rhymes about cats and mice; felt-tipped pens.

Preparation
Make a copy of the photocopiable sheet for each child. Display several nursery rhyme books on a low table with the pages open on traditional cat and mouse rhymes. Read and learn rhymes with the children such as 'Pussy Cat, Pussy Cat', 'Ding, Dong, Bell' and 'Three Blind Mice'.

What to do
Gather the children together to warm up. Ask them to curl up and pretend to be asleep on the floor. Invite them to wake up and stretch. Repeat, reminding the children to stretch hands, fingers, feet and toes.

Demonstrate how a cat stretches. Invite the children to balance on their hands and knees, gently lift their heads up as they dip their backs, then slowly arch their backs as they lower their heads to look at the floor.

Invite a child to curl up like a sleeping cat. Take the other children to a space. Ask them to pretend to be mice hiding in their mouse hole. Challenge the mice to venture out of the hole to explore. Encourage them to creep quietly towards the cat.

Tell the children that when you call out 'Cat's coming!', the cat should wake up and chase the mice back to their hole. For a fun ending, chase all the children back to their hole.

Gather the children together and invite them to calm down at the end of the session by doing

five or six cat stretches. Sing the nursery rhymes and talk about the activity with the children. Carry out the activity over several weeks so that each child has a turn to be the cat.

Individual recording
Give each child a copy of the photocopiable sheet. Ask them to draw the mice in different hiding places such as in the mouse hole, under the chair or behind the plant.

Support
Provide support for younger children as they complete their photocopiable sheets by encouraging them to draw each mouse.

Extension
Invite older children to draw their own hiding places, such as inside a shoe or under a table.

Assessment
Note whether the children can move slowly and quietly during the game. Can they move quickly? Can they keep still? Can they take on the role of the cat? Note whether the children are able to move safely. Can they recall the activity?

Home links
Ask parents and carers to sing cat and mouse rhymes with their children at home and to point out cats moving, stretching and sleeping.

Cat's coming!

Row the boat

Learning objective
To move with confidence, imagination and in safety when working co-operatively with others.

Group size
Eight children.

What you need
The photocopiable sheet; large, safe space; felt-tipped pens.

Preparation
Make a copy of the photocopiable sheet for each child. Learn the words of the traditional song 'Row, Row, Row Your Boat' in *This Little Puffin...* compiled by Elizabeth Matterson (Puffin Books).

What to do
Sing the song together, gently rocking from side to side. Divide the children into pairs. Encourage them to explore different ways of sitting together to row their boat. Suggest that they could sit back to back, face to back, side by side or facing each other.

Challenge the children to make up their own actions to the words 'Row, row, row your boat, gently down the Nile; if you see a crocodile, don't forget to smile'. Repeat for the words 'Row, row, row your boat, gently down the stream; if you see a crocodile, don't forget to scream' and 'Row, row, row your boat, gently to and fro; swish, swash, swish, swash, over the side we go'.

Encourage the children to mirror each other's actions of rocking, smiling, screaming, falling over the side of the boat, splashing and swimming around as if being chased by a crocodile.

Gradually build up the number of children working together until the whole group creates one large boat.

Ask the children to make up their own words and actions to the tune.

Invite the children to calm down at the end of the session by repeating the first verse of the song, quietly rocking together. Then talk about the activity with the children while they are sitting down.

Individual recording
Give each child a copy of the photocopiable sheet. Encourage them to draw a picture of themselves in the boat doing one of the actions from the song.

Support
Build up the numbers of children in one large boat over a period of weeks. Provide suggestions for younger children to draw their favourite actions on their photocopiable sheets.

Extension
Encourage older children to make up their own verses and actions, and record these on the back of their photocopiable sheets. Use these when reviewing the activity.

Assessment
Note whether the children can match their actions to the words of the song. Can they make up their own words and create their own movement ideas? Note whether the children rock with a partner side to side, back to back, face to back or facing each other. Can they work in small groups of four or eight?

Home links
Invite parents and carers to practise the song with their children at home to help them learn the words.

Row the boat

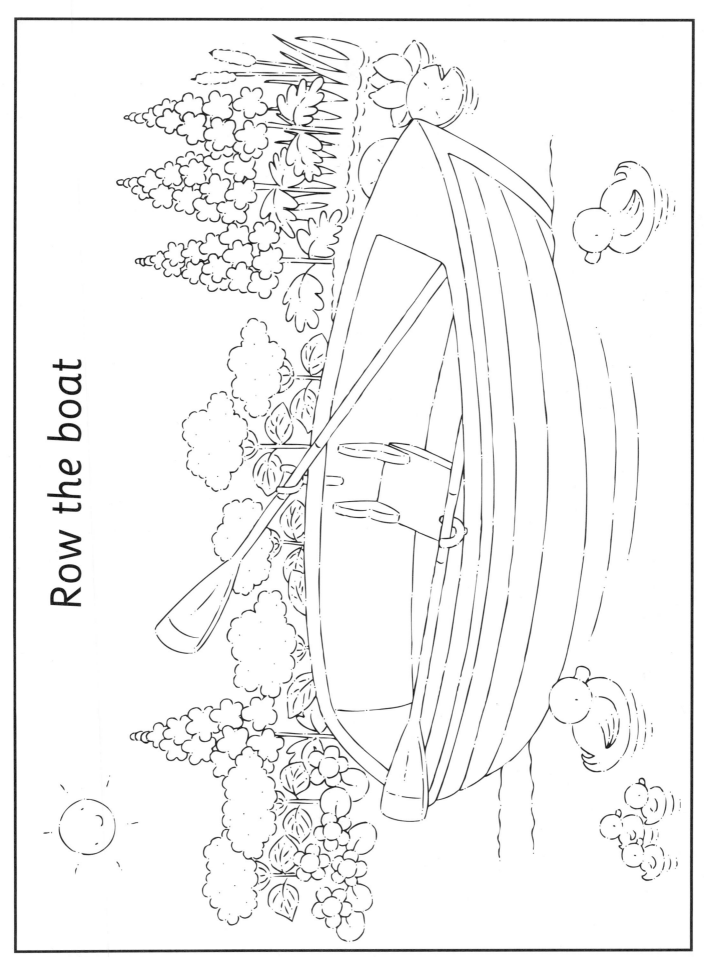

Streamers in space

Learning objective
To move with control and co-ordination using streamers to explore pathways in space and on the floor.

Group size
Any size.

What you need
The photocopiable sheet; large, safe space; tape recorder; tape of gentle music such as traditional Chinese music or music by Vangelis; two brightly-coloured streamers for each child; felt-tipped pens.

Preparation
Make a copy of the photocopiable sheet for each child. Set up the tape recorder ready to play.

What to do
Sit with the children on the floor to listen to the music. Encourage them to warm up by moving gently to the music. Then invite them to stand up and stretch out in every possible direction.

Encourage the children to travel around the room exploring different pathways. Ask them to move in straight lines, diagonally and in curvy, twisting movements. Challenge them to change direction by turning and spinning around. Allow time for free exploration.

Gather the children together and demonstrate how to use the streamers, then give each child two brightly-coloured streamers. Ask them to wave them high in the air, in front of their body, to either side, behind, at waist height, near to the floor and along it to make different patterns.

Replay the music. Challenge the children to move around the room using the streamers to create straight and wavy pathways along the floor and in the air. Remind the children to take care not to bump into one another. Encourage them to practise and make minor changes to improve their repeatable dance patterns.

Gather the children together and collect the streamers. Invite the children to calm down at the end of the session by standing up and gently stretching their arms to the limits of their personal space. Ask them to sit down and talk about the activity together.

Individual recording
Give each child a copy of the photocopiable sheet. Ask them to record their dance by drawing streamers in different positions around the central body shape.

Support
Let younger children use one streamer at a time and draw just two streamers on their photocopiable sheets.

Extension
Invite older children to record on their photocopiable sheets the pathways and patterns that they created when dancing with the streamers. Encourage them to use the drawings when reviewing the activity.

Assessment
Note whether the children listen and respond to instructions. Can they make a variety of pathways across the floor? Can they make different pathways in the air? Note whether the children make up repeatable dance patterns? Can they show their dance to others?

Home links
Invite parents and carers to come in to watch their children perform the streamer dance.

Streamers in space

Where's Jack?

Learning objective
To travel in different directions to create a dance based on the story of 'Jack and the Beanstalk'.

Group size
Any size

What you need
The photocopiable sheet; large, safe space; the story or knowledge of 'Jack and the Beanstalk'; felt-tipped pens.

Preparation
Make a copy of the photocopiable sheet for each child. Familiarize the children with the story of 'Jack and the Beanstalk'.

What to do
Gather the children together. Give them some imaginary bean seeds to plant. Invite them to pretend that they are the beans growing upwards until they can stretch no higher. Repeat this several times.

Ask the children to stand far away from the imaginary beanstalk. Invite them to find different ways of creeping towards the beanstalk and climbing up it, taking care not to wake the giant. Explain to the children that when you call out the word 'Giant!', they must run back taking long, heavy footsteps. Ask them questions such as, 'How can you reach the beanstalk without the giant seeing you?', 'How can you get back quickly?' and so on.

Encourage the children to move in different directions such as forwards, backwards and to the right and left. Explain that they can move in a straight line or zigzag along in a wavy pathway or twisting along a curling spiral pathway. Invite them to create their own ways of moving.

Divide the children into three groups. Challenge one group to be beanstalks growing upwards and falling to the ground when chopped; the second group of children to portray Jack's actions of planting seeds, climbing up and down the beanstalk and running away from the giant, and the third group to move like the giant. Encourage the children to work together to the story through movement. Let them freely explore all roles.

At the end of the session, gather the children together to talk about the activity.

Individual recording
Give each child a copy of the photocopiable sheet. Ask them to help Jack find his way back to the beanstalk. Encourage them to trace the path with their finger, talking about the different directions that they can take. When they have found the correct path, invite them to draw it with a pencil.

Support
Carry out the activity over a few weeks with younger children. Encourage them to describe the activity in their own words.

Extension
Challenge older children to draw their own maze for Jack to find the beanstalk.

Assessment
Note how the children move. Can they move forwards? Can they move from side to side? Note if the children move backwards safely. Are they able to move like the beanstalk, Jack and the giant?

Home links
Invite the children to tell their parents and carers the story of 'Jack and the Beanstalk' in their own words.

Where's Jack?

Teddy lost, Teddy found

Learning objective
To show awareness of space, of themselves and of others by adjusting speed or changing direction using the stimulus of a teddy.

Group size
Any size.

What you need
The photocopiable sheet; large, safe space; the children's teddies; felt-tipped pens.

Preparation
Make a copy of the photocopiable sheet for each child. Ask the children to bring in a teddy each. Invite them to show and talk about their teddies during circle time. Read the rhyme 'Teddy Bear, Teddy Bear' in *This Little Puffin…* compiled by Elizabeth Matterson (Puffin Books).

What to do
Gather the children in a circle with their teddies. Explain that the teddies are going to join them for movement and that they have to warm up, too. Encourage the children to do actions to some of the words in the rhyme, for example, touch the teddies' noses, bend down and touch toes, curl up on the floor with the teddies and twirl around with the teddies on the spot.

Tell the children that they are going to 'lose' their teddies when they take them for a walk around the room. When you call out 'Teddy lost!', it is the signal for the children to drop their teddies before continuing on their way. Ask the children to look around the room for their lost teddies. Call out 'Teddy found!' as a signal for them to find their teddies and bring them back home. Walk through the activity with the children initially to give them an idea of the actions.

Repeat the activity several times using different pathways, different ways of moving, and different speeds.

Gather the children in a circle again. Repeat the teddy rhymes and actions that they made up at the beginning of the activity to help them calm down both mentally and physically. Ask them to sit down and gently cuddle their teddies as they are happy to be reunited with them. Talk with the children about the activity, pointing out some of the different pathways that they took on their journey.

Individual task
Give each child a copy of the photocopiable sheet. Invite them to link up pictures of themselves with the teddies to record the activity on the chart.

Support
Ask younger children to describe the activity in their own words. Support them as they fill in their charts.

Extension
Encourage older children to make up a story to go with the actions, demonstrating the activity to the rest of the group.

Assessment
Note which children listen and respond to instructions. Can they talk about their teddy to others? Can they describe their feelings when Teddy is lost and when Teddy is found?

Home links
Ask parents and carers to encourage their children to look for lost possessions themselves.

Teddy lost, Teddy found

Musical mats

Learning objective
To gain an understanding of personal space.

Group size
Any size.

What you need
The photocopiable sheet; large, safe space; floor mats; tambourine or piece of upbeat music; felt-tipped pens.

Preparation
Make a copy of the photocopiable sheet for each child. Talk to the children about the benefits of maintaining a safe personal space during circle time, and let them help to get the mats out and ready.

What to do
Invite the children to each sit quietly by themselves on a mat. Explain that the mat is their special place (personal space). Challenge them to explore their personal space by reaching out as far as possible in all directions from a sitting position on the mat. Repeat from a lying-down position. Ask the children to stand on their mats and encourage them to reach out on all levels and in all directions to explore the space around them.

Invite the children to move freely around the space between the mats, taking care not to step on them or bump into one another. Tell them that when you say 'Stop!', they should return to their mats to make statue-like shapes. Repeat

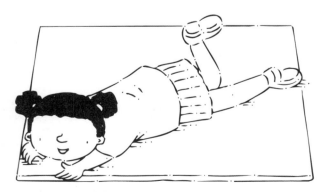

several times to encourage the use of different levels and stretches.

Develop the activity by using a tambourine or by starting and stopping a piece of upbeat music. At the end of the session, invite the children to return to a quiet sitting position on their mats and talk about the activity.

Individual recording
Give each child a copy of the photocopiable sheet. Invite them to complete the picture of themselves in a 'freeze' position and to use the blank space to draw a picture of themselves making a stretched shape on the mat.

Support
Help younger children to understand the concepts by talking about the pictures on the photocopiable sheet. Let them observe the other children with you pointing out good ideas that they could try themselves.

Extension
Invite older children to demonstrate their ideas to the rest of the group.

Assessment
Note the way that the children carry the mat to a space. Can they return to their mat on the 'Stop!' command? Note whether the children are able to move safely between the mats without stepping on them. Are they able to make different body shapes on their mat? Note whether the children use different levels. Do they show an understanding of the concept of personal space?

Home links
Invite the children to ask their parents and carers to find a place for them at home which can be their special space, such as a corner of a room, a hiding place behind a settee or a small rug under a table. Ask parents and carers to give their children sole responsibility, within reason, for what happens in this personal space.

Musical mats

Flyaway feathers

Learning objective
To recognize the changes that happen to their bodies when they are active, using feathers as props for dance involving the levels of high, medium and low.

Group size
Small groups of six to eight children.

What you need
The photocopiable sheet; large, safe space; tape of gentle music such as 'The Swan' from *Carnival of the Animals* by Saint-Saëns; bag of brightly-coloured feathers; felt-tipped pens.

Preparation
Make a copy of the photocopiable sheet for each child. Show the children the bag of feathers and discuss them at circle time. Lead the children in warm-up activities to stretch to the limits of their personal space.

What to do
Ask the children to sit down. Show them how to inhale through their noses and how to blow gently through their mouths. Encourage them to practise on their own. Show them how to feel their breath on their hands as they breathe in and out.

Show the children the bag of feathers. Take one feather out of the bag and ask the group to watch. Blow the feather very gently up into the air. Invite the children to recall what happens as the feather descends to the ground.

Play some gentle music. Give each child a feather and challenge them to keep it up in the air by blowing while the music plays. Stop the music and ask the children to let their feathers fall gently to the floor with them to rest. Repeat several times. Encourage the children to notice how their tummies move up and down, how they feel hot and breathe faster when active, and how their breath gets slower when they are resting.

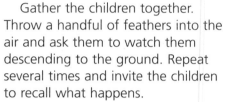

Gather the children together. Throw a handful of feathers into the air and ask them to watch them descending to the ground. Repeat several times and invite the children to recall what happens.

Give each child several feathers and let them explore them freely. Encourage them to throw them high into the air and watch them as they fall to the floor. Collect the feathers back into the bag. Cool down at the end of the session by repeating the slow breathing. Turn off the music and talk about the activity.

Individual task
Give each child a photocopiable sheet. Invite them to colour in the feathers, then help them to follow the diagram at the bottom of the page to make a feather spinner. Encourage them to stretch up tall and drop their feather spinner, then watch it twirling to the ground.

Support
Provide younger children with plenty of support as they make their feather spinners.

Extension
Encourage older children to make up a twirling sequence based on the movements of their feather spinners. What happens to their breathing when they spin and twirl?

Assessment
Note whether the children can keep the feathers in the air by blowing them. Can they blow them along the ground? Can they explain what happens to their bodies when they breathe in and out?

Home links
Invite the children to show their parents and carers how to practise slow breathing at home when they relax together. Encourage them to look for feathered animals in books or around their environment.

Flyaway feathers

Bursting bubbles

Learning objective
To experience the contrasting qualities of sustained, fine touch and quick strong movements based on the life cycle of a bubble.

Group size
Any size.

What you need
The photocopiable sheet; large, safe space; some bubble mixture and a wand.

Preparation
Make a copy of the photocopiable sheet for each child. Prepare some bubble mixture.

What to do
Blow some bubbles and invite the children to observe them floating and bursting. Encourage the children to follow the bubbles and jump to catch them as they go up in the air. Challenge the children to each try to catch a bubble on the palm of their hand.

Invite the children to imitate the way a bubble floats in the air until it gently comes to rest before bursting. Ask them to repeat the movement phrases so that they are all floating and popping like a burst of bubbles. Encourage the children to move in and out of one another as if they were each gently holding a bubble on the palm of their hand.

Tell the children that when you clap they should pretend to be bubbles bursting. Challenge the children to jump high, springing up and outwards in spiky movements. Encourage them to make appropriate noises to highlight the contrasts in movements. Repeat the movements in sequence to form a dance.

Individual recording
Give each child a copy of the photocopiable sheet. Encourage them to complete the bubbles by placing their pencil on the dot and following the dotted lines. This will help to develop fine motor skills and pencil control.

Support
Let younger children observe the activity. Hold the wand for them while they blow the mixture.

Extension
Challenge older children to create a dance sequence together, one taking on the role of the floating bubble while the other imitates the bubble bursting.

Assessment
Note whether the children observe the bubbles. Can they follow a bubble? Can they attempt to catch a bubble on an outstretched palm? Note whether the children are able to imitate the contrasting movements of bubbles floating in the air or settling as they burst? Can they create a dance sequence of the contrasting bubble movements?

Home links
Ask parents and carers to help their children to discover other floating objects such as feathers, airborne seeds, soapsuds and dust particles. Invite them to encourage their children to observe how gently they move around in the air.

Bursting bubbles

Follow the tin robot

Learning objective
To move like a robot while repeating actions with improving skill.

Group size
Four to six children.

What you need
The photocopiable sheet; metal items; cardboard box big enough to fit over a child's head; tin foil; shiny paper; milk-bottle tops; pipe-cleaners; scissors; glue; large, safe space.

Preparation
Make a copy of the photocopiable sheet for each child. Help the children to cover the box with tin foil. Cut out a large square where the child's face will appear, so that it is not covered. Invite the children to decorate the box to look like a robot's head with shiny paper and milk-bottle tops, and to stick on features such as pipe-cleaner antennae.

What to do
Discuss the mechanical features of robots and the repetitive motions of machines. Show the children some metal objects to touch and feel so that they can understand the unyielding nature of metal. Demonstrate how a robot might move with jerky, mechanical movements.

Encourage the children to take turns to wear the robot's head and practise talking and moving like a robot. Invite them to take turns to lead the others in a dance around the room using the repetitive, stiff mechanical movements of a robot.

Individual recording
Give each child a copy of the photocopiable sheet. Encourage them to colour the corresponding body part and tick the appropriate box when they have made their own body part move like a robot.

Support
Let younger children observe the movements of the others. If they wish, they can invent their own versions of robotic movements rather than copy others. If they are reluctant to wear the robot's head and lead the dance, take them by the hand while gently holding the robot's head in place.

Extension
Encourage older children to make up repeatable dance phrases for the other children to follow. They could also perform the robot dance for others to watch.

Assessment
Note whether the children are confident enough to wear the robot's head. Are they able to move stiffly like a robot? Are they able to make up a series of repetitive movements? Note whether the children follow the lead of others. Can they lead the dance?

Home links
Ask parents and carers to point out mechanical objects in the home and on the television, and to highlight the repetitiveness of machine movements such as cogs and pendulums.

Follow the tin robot

head ☐   body ☐   legs ☐

arms ☐   hands ☐   feet ☐

Rhythm sticks

Learning objective
To handle objects safely and with increasing control when matching movement to the beats that a partner makes with rhythm sticks.

Group size
Eight or ten children.

What you need
The photocopiable sheet; large, safe space; saw (adult use); bamboo canes; two rhythm sticks; felt-tipped pens.

Preparation
Make a copy of the photocopiable sheet for each child. Make a pair of rhythm sticks for each child by sawing bamboo canes into short lengths. Use them to accompany songs at circle time so that the children get accustomed to handling them safely and within boundaries suited to individual settings.

What to do
Ask the children to sit on the floor. Show them the rhythm sticks and demonstrate different beats. Give each child a pair of rhythm sticks and let them experiment for a few minutes. Ask them to beat out the sound pattern of their name, for example, 'Jo-anne', 'Sam-an-deep', 'O-liv-ia' or 'Tom'. Demonstrate how to beat the sticks together slowly, quickly and using a combination of the two speeds.

Divide the children into pairs. Let them take it in turns to use the rhythm sticks to beat out simple, repeatable rhymes and then to tap out two or three beat rhythms. Encourage them to play the rhythms slowly, quickly and using a combination of the two speeds. Invite the children to take it in turns to copy each other's rhythms. Challenge them to use the sticks as if they were having a conversation. Point out different rhythms for them to recognize and

repeat. Invite the children to match movement to the sound patterns to encourage them to move rhythmically.

Ask one child to beat out slow 'clicks' on the rhythm sticks to represent walking, and the other child to respond to the beat with the corresponding movement. Repeat and encourage changes of pace.

Individual recording
Give each child a copy of the photocopiable sheet to record their responses to the activity. Ask them to tick the boxes next to playing fast, playing slow, a combination of the two speeds, moving fast, moving slow and a combination of the two when they have achieved them.

Support
Let younger children use the rhythm sticks as they move freely around the room.

Extension
Ask older children to demonstrate their movements to the rest of the group.

Assessment
Note whether the children can hold the rhythm sticks correctly and use them safely. Can the children tap out the syllables of their names? Note whether the children take the lead. Do they follow? Can they repeat a one/two/three beat rhythm? Can they make movements to accompany the clacks of their own/others sticks? Note whether the children can repeat the movement phase. Can they demonstrate to the rest of the group?

Home links
Give each child a copy of the completed photocopiable sheet to take home. Ask parents and carers to help their children practise and perfect the movements that they made during the activity at your setting.

Rhythm sticks

☐ play fast	
☐ move fast	
☐ play slow	
☐ move slow	
☐ play fast and slow	
☐ move fast and slow	

My beautiful balloon

Learning objective
To handle a balloon carefully and with increasing control as stimulus for movement.

Group size
Four to six children.

What you need
The photocopiable sheet; large, safe space; round balloons; large bin liner; felt-tipped pens.

Preparation
Make a copy of the photocopiable sheet for each child. Blow up the balloons and place them inside a large bin liner until you are ready to use them.

What to do
Explain to the children that they are going to use the balloons for movement and that they can play freely with them later. Give each child a balloon. Tell them that they must look at it and hold it with two hands at all times. Encourage them to gently feel the surface of the balloon. Invite them to lift the balloon high into the air, looking at it all the time. Ask them to move the balloon all around their body without letting it go or without looking at it. Suggest that they

move the balloon near the floor, above their head, in front, behind, to one side of their body, to the other side and so on.

Challenge the children to find ways of moving along the floor without letting go of their balloons. Emphasize the importance of keeping the balloons under control and near to their bodies. At the end of the session, allow the children a couple of minutes free play with their balloons, then ask them to each gently hold their balloon in two hands and sit down with it.

Individual recording
Give each child a copy of the photocopiable sheet. Ask them to draw a different face on each balloon to show where their eyes were focused when moving with the balloon, for example, in front, up in the air, down to the ground, to the left and to the right. Invite them to draw their own idea in the spare balloon.

Support
Let younger children use the photocopiable sheet to help them describe what happened during the activity.

Extension
Encourage older children to use the photocopiable sheet to record other ways that they moved with their balloons.

Assessment
Note whether the children can hold the balloon with two hands. Can the children control the balloon? Can they keep the balloon close to the body? Note whether the children focus on the balloon throughout the activity. Can they move the balloon in front, up, down, behind and to the side of the body on command? Can they follow and retrieve a balloon safely?

Home links
Ask parents and carers to carry out similar activities at home using different-sized balls to encourage development of positional language.

My beautiful balloon

Blanket play

Learning objective

To use their imagination while using a blanket as a prop to create a dance with a partner.

Group size

Eight or ten children.

What you need

The photocopiable sheet; large, safe space; brightly-coloured blankets.

Preparation

Gather the children together and explain to them the boundaries for the activity and the safety issues about using a blanket with a partner. Remind them how important it is to be gentle and to care for one another during relationship play. Divide the children into pairs and give each pair a blanket to share, to use as a prop to create a dance. Ask them to hold the edges and shake it together. Make a copy of the photocopiable sheet for each child.

What to do

Invite the pairs of children to try out different ways of using a blanket to make up a dance composition with a beginning, a middle and an end. Encourage the children to pretend that the blanket is their home. Tell them that they are going to make up a dance with their partner about moving house. Invite them to find a space on the floor and wrap themselves up in the blanket as it is night-time. Encourage them to wake up, yawn and stretch their arms, then wander around looking for another place to live so that they can have a bigger home together.

Finish by asking each pair of children to take the blanket to another space and to wrap up and quietly hide from the world. Collect the blankets and talk about the activity.

Individual recording

Give each child a copy of the photocopiable sheet and ask them to try out some of the ways that the blanket can be used. Invite them to talk about what is happening in each picture and to work with a partner for the shared activities.

Support

Encourage younger children to work with older partners who would be responsible for caring for them.

Extension

Challenge older children to find different ways of moving with the blanket and to make up their own story line.

Home links

Ask parents and carers to let their children have any old blankets to use for movement or to build dens with at home.

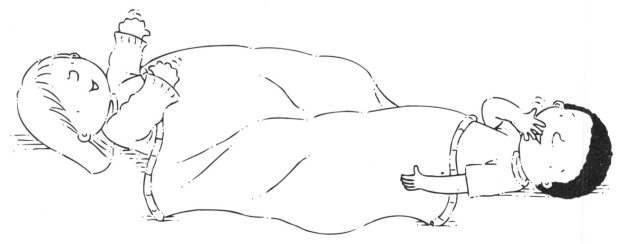

Blanket play

Yellow submarine

Learning objective
To express and communicate ideas, thoughts and feelings through movement by working in a group to create a dance about a submarine.

Group size
Six or eight children.

What you need
The photocopiable sheet; tape recorder or CD player; copy of 'Yellow Submarine' from *Yellow Submarine* by the Beatles (Apple), on tape or CD; large, safe space; selection of felt-tipped pens.

Preparation
Make a copy of the photocopiable sheet for each child. Look at books with stories and pictures of submarines and learn the words to the song 'Yellow Submarine'.

What to do
Gather the children together and tell them that they are going to make up a dance about life on board a submarine. Challenge the children to find different ways of moving, linked to the submarine theme – for example, they could move up and down like the periscope, salute the captain, hold their noses to go under water or glide through the water.

Encourage the children to think of their own ideas and let them show these individually. Point out some good ways of moving. Invite the children to demonstrate their favourite movements. Set the children's favourite actions to the music by practising them several times until the children can repeat them. Help them to improve their dance by suggesting minor changes such as moments of stillness or dancing the same repetitive pattern at different times.

At the end of the session, gently sing and rock to the music, as if sailing on a submarine.

Individual recording
Give each child a copy of the photocopiable sheet and ask them to record their movements by colouring each part of the submarine when they have achieved the action indicated. Invite them to make up and record their own ideas in the blank spaces.

Support
Let younger children observe the finished group dance. Support them as they complete their photocopiable sheets and encourage them to explain what they can see.

Extension
Challenge older children to work together to make up their own dance patterns. Encourage them to use their photocopiable sheets as information and posters to advertise a performance of the dance, sticking them on the walls around your setting.

Assessment
Note whether the children can make up a dance about the submarine. Can the children improve their actions by repeating them? Can they move in time to the music? Note whether the children work alone or with others in the group. Can they recall the story using words and actions?

Home links
Give parents and carers a copy of their children's completed photocopiable sheets and ask them to help their children practise the individual movements at home so that they can repeat the actions for a performance.

Yellow submarine

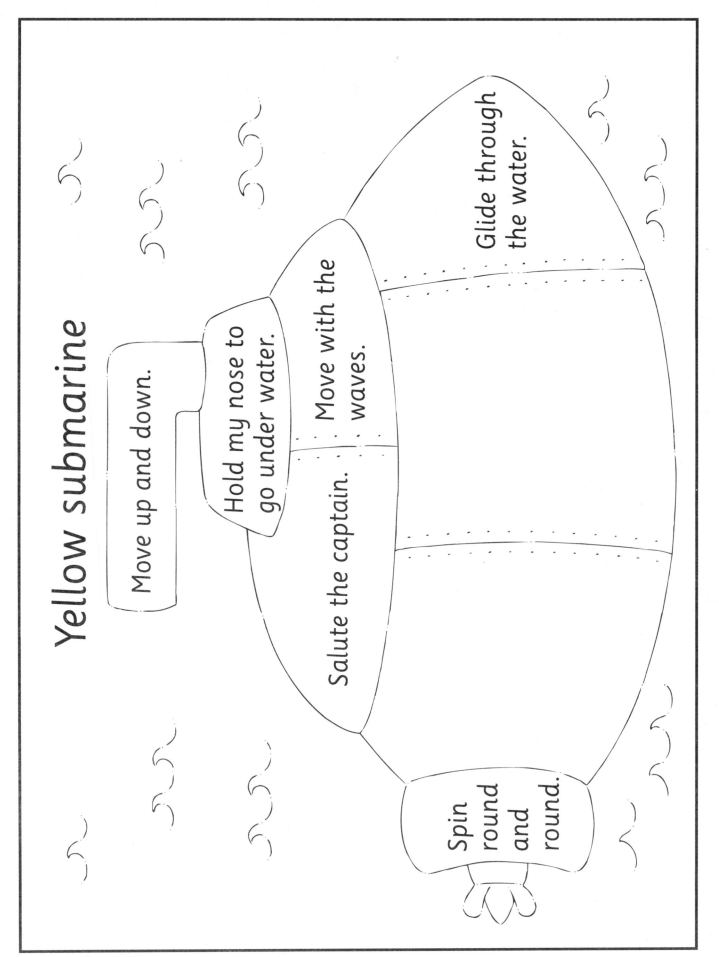

Move up and down.

Hold my nose to go under water.

Move with the waves.

Glide through the water.

Salute the captain.

Spin round and round.

Name _____

Skills development chart

I can travel in different directions to create a dance

I can adjust speed or change direction using a teddy

I can show awareness of personal space

I can explore pathways in space and on the floor using streamers

I can use my imagination while using a blanket as a prop to create a dance with a partner

I can recognize the changes that happen to my body when it is active

I can work co-operatively with others

I can express and communicate ideas, thoughts and feelings through a dance about a submarine

I can handle a balloon carefully with increasing control

I can use fine touch and quick strong movements based on a bubble

I can use the contrasting speeds of fast and slow

I can match movement to the beats of rhythm sticks

I can move like a robot while repeating actions

I can move safely and stop on command

◪ SCHOLASTIC   Skills for early years Dance and movement

25 Ways To Say No!

A Floral Colouring Book For

STRESSED-OUT

Teaching Assistants

The Art Of Saying 'No'

Firstly, thank you for buying this book. I hope you enjoy many calm hours colouring it in! Just a quick note: I've deliberately left the reverse of each page blank, to avoid any bleeding of colours, front to back.

The art of saying 'no' is in making the person, doing the asking, feel appreciated. Although there are 25 ways to say 'no', in this book, not every way will suit you and your personality.

YOU are a unique individual, so choose only those phrases that feel like a good fit for you. Then practice them, over and over, in your mind and aloud in those rare moments when you find yourself alone.

We humans are creatures of habit, so by habituating your chosen, new ways of saying 'no', to your subconscious brain, they'll be much easier to say when the need arises.

Saying 'no' doesn't have to be difficult. It just depends on how you choose to do it and how much you value yourself and your time.

If you'd like to learn more ways to make your life run more smoothly and seamlessly, go to taincontrol.com   love

I appreciate the invitation but I've got too much on to be of use.

Thanks so much
for thinking of me,
but reluctantly,
I'll have to decline.

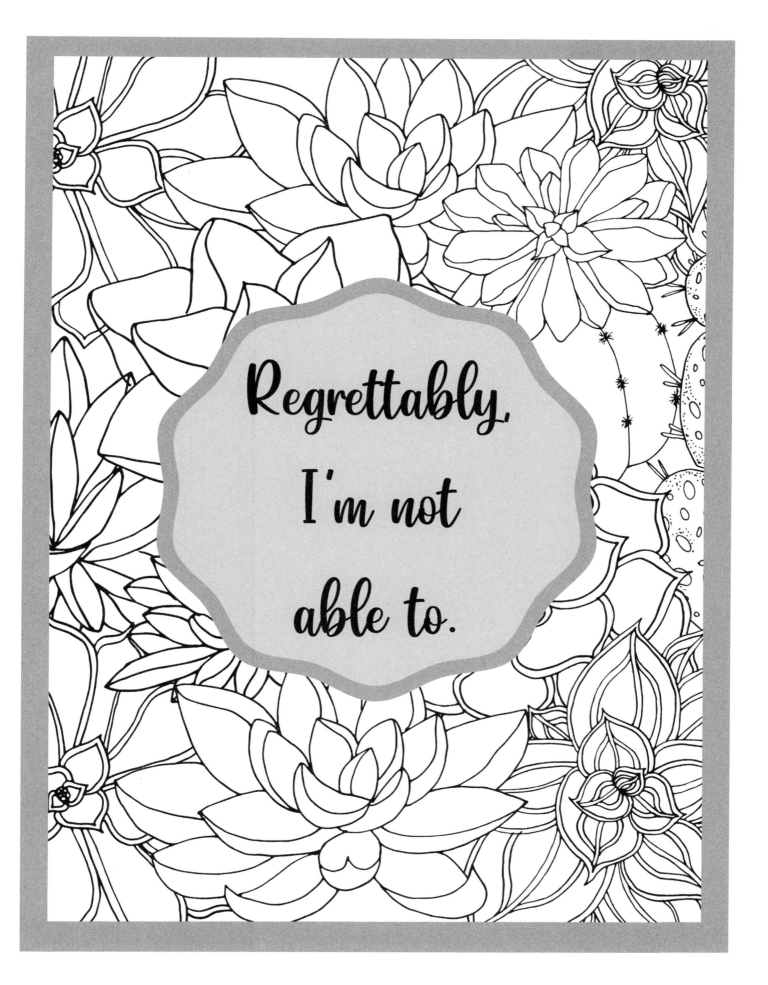

Thank you so much, maybe another time.

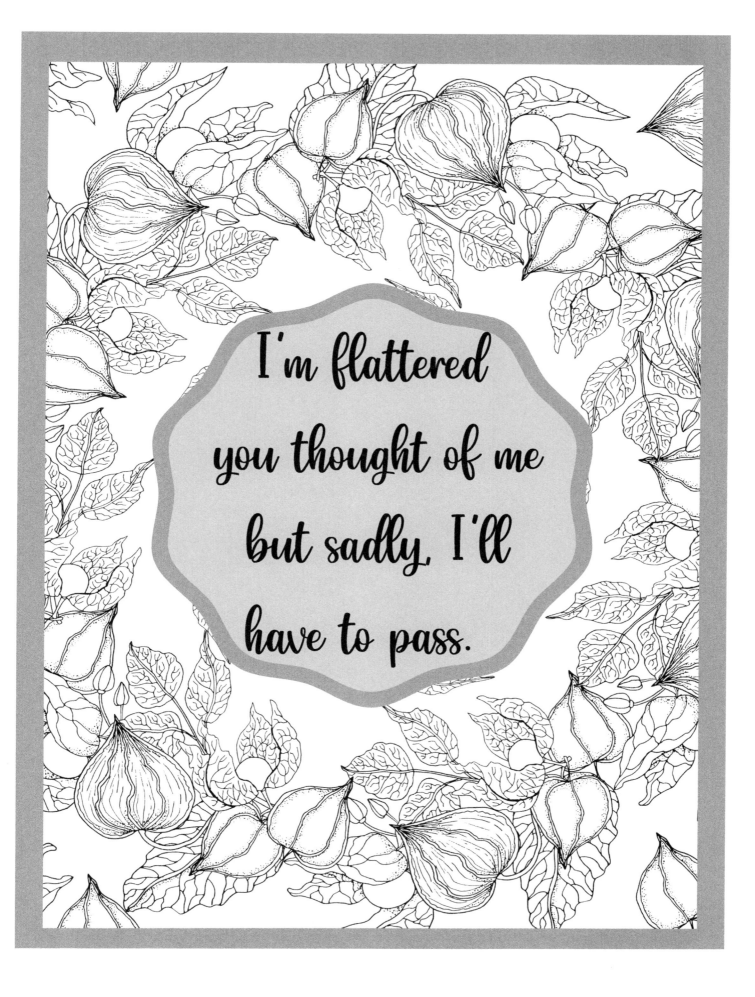

It sounds great but I won't be able to make the commitment.

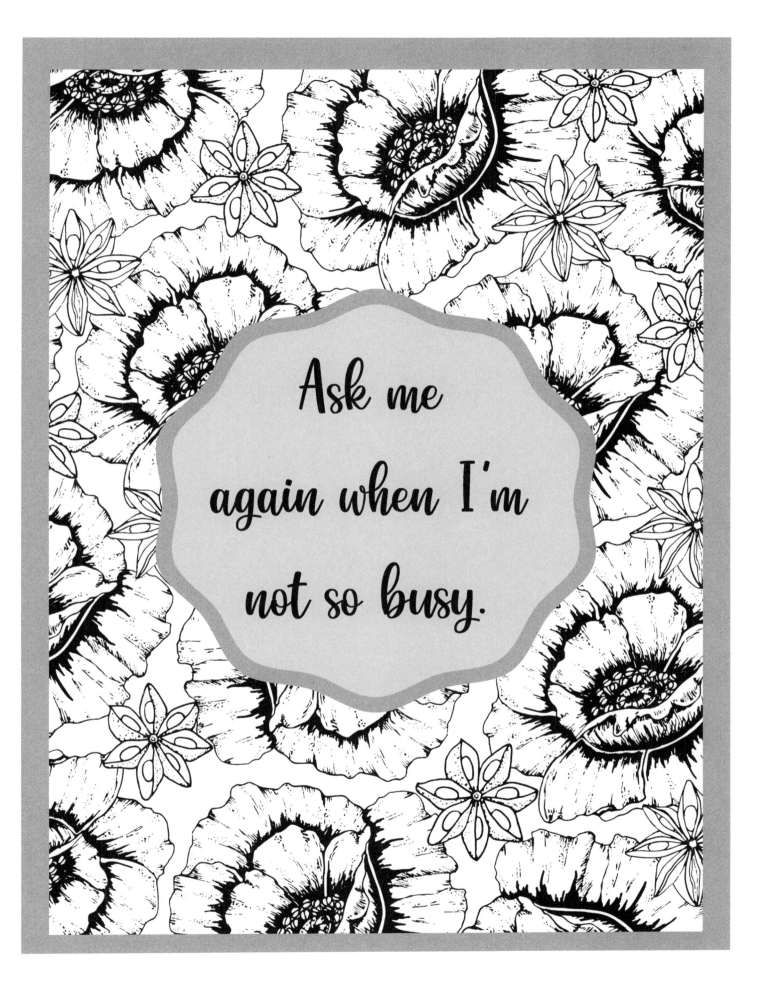

Perhaps in a few weeks when things have slowed down a bit.

Let me think about it and I'll get back to you.

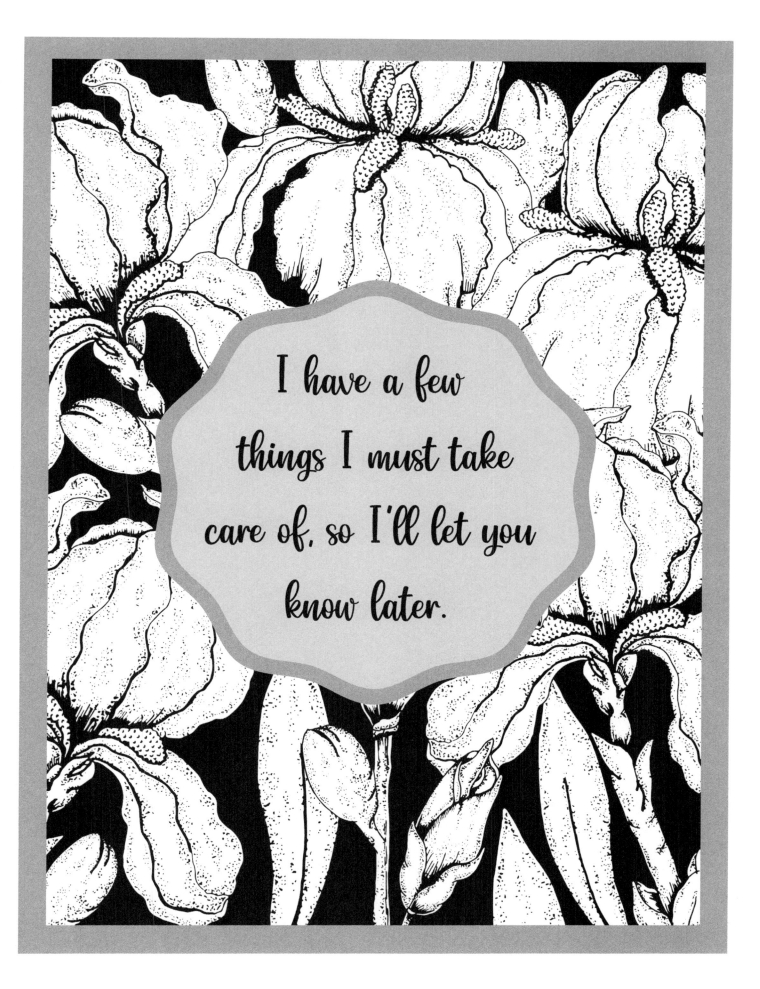

I have a few things I must take care of, so I'll let you know later.

I wish I could,
but I can't take
on any more
right now.

If only there were two of me, I'd be able to help.

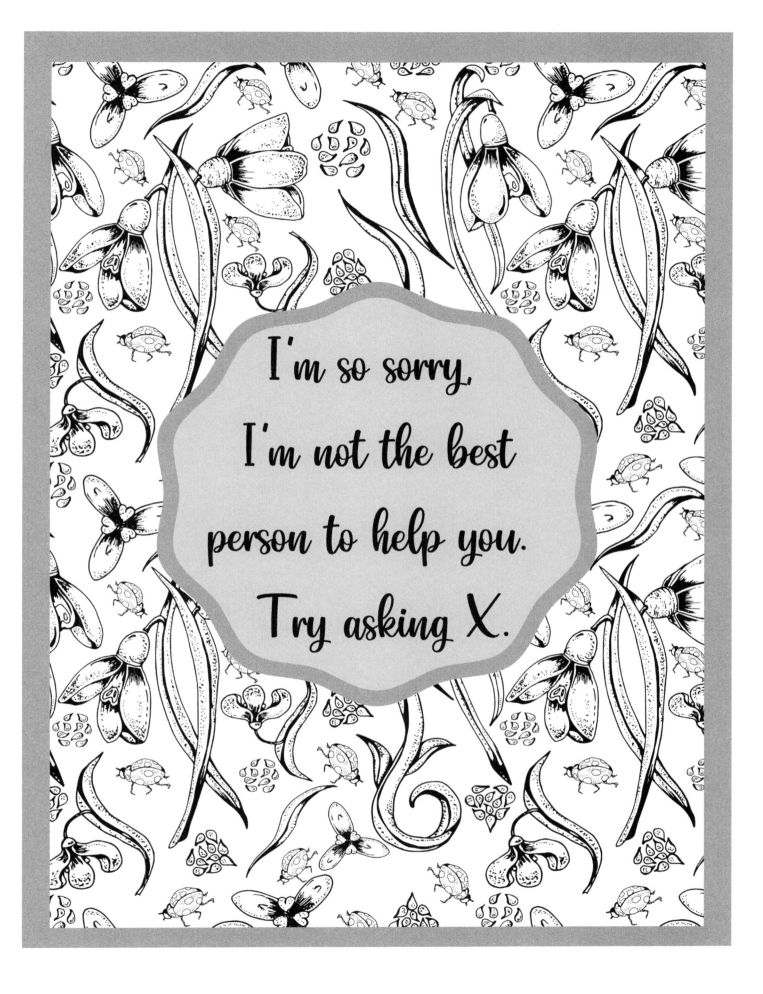

I'm so sorry, I'm not the best person to help you. Try asking X.

Apologies,
but I can't
make it.

My children will never forgive me if I don't get home on time today.

Sorry, I'm notoriously unsociable, but I hope you all have a brilliant time!

Cut this page out
and put it
between your pages
whilst colouring
to reduce bleeding
of colours
from one page
to the next!

I hope you are enjoying this book!

Please tell other Teaching Assistants about my books so that I get to help as many TAs as possible make their day just a little bit easier!

To see all of my TA IN CONTROL books, please scan the QR code or type www.taincontrol.com/books into your browser. Thank you!